30 SELECTED DUETS

FOR TWO SAXOPHONES

(Easy-Intermediate)

Compiled and Edited by

JAY ARNOLD

These duets have been compiled from the works of masters of composition who have given special significance to the importance of the Clarinet in the world of music.

They are excellent preparatory material for the advanced stages. Each player should diligently practice his part in solo form before associating the performance with the other part.

CONTENTS

© Copyright 1975 by Edward Schuberth & Co., Inc.
263 Veterans Boulevard, Carlstadt, N.J. 07072
International Copyright Secured   Made in U.S.A.

TEN DUETS

H. KLOSE

3

4

Allegro non troppo

3

Andante

molto sostenuto

5

14

D. C. al Fine

Moderato non troppo

légèremente

23

Allegro giusto

28

Andantino sostenuto

10

TEN DUETS

A. MAYEUR

30

Allegro moderato

2

Moderato

3

34

Andante moderato

38

Andante

7

Allegretto

Allegro

9

46

TEN DUETS

J. SELLNER

Adagio con espressione

54

.59

Siciliano

5

62

Allegro moderato

ASHLEY PUBLICATIONS INC.

Lewis Music Publishing Co., Inc.

present

an elaborate library of music for the

CLASSIC GUITAR

WF 43   **SOLOS FOR CLASSIC GUITAR**
Original transcriptions compiled and edited by Harvey Vinson.
A collection of the finest works ever written for the instrument.

WF 45   **CARCASSI METHOD**
English and Spanish text, edited by Harvey Vinson.

MATTEO CARCASSI (32 studies in original form)

WF 56   **SELECTED MASTERPIECES FOR THE CLASSIC GUITAR (VOL. I)**
Compiled and edited by Frantz Casseus. Expands the literature
of WF 43 with celebrated transcriptions and original works of
Sor, Aguado, Giuliani, Tarrega and others.

SELECTED MASTERPIECES FOR THE CLASSIC GUITAR (VOL. II)

GRADED ANTHOLOGY FOR CLASSIC GUITAR
A marvelous introduction to the instrument and its pioneer
composers, by Walter Kaye Bauer, the answer to "what, when
and where" to get the student started, advanced and enthused.

FAMILIAR MUSIC FOR THE CLASSIC GUITAR
Compiled and arranged by Walter Kaye Bauer. Includes not
only the works of the masters but many familiar tunes hitherto
unavailable for the classic guitar.

MORE FAMILIAR MUSIC FOR THE CLASSIC GUITAR
A second volume embodying the above description.

UP-TO-DATE METHOD FOR CLASSIC GUITAR
Prepared by Fred Nance and Mary Godla who have endowed
this method with the benefit of many years of teaching expe-
rience. Will fill the needs of early grade students.

PRIMER FOR THE CLASSIC GUITAR
The most elementary of our classic guitar publications, by the
authors of the Up-To-Date Method, designed for begi
the earliest stages of instruction.

DISTRIBUTED BY HAL LEONARD

0 73999 10557 5
00510557   U.S. $7.95

ISBN-13: 978-1-4234-4106-9

50795

9 781423 441069